Stan is your normal 3rd grade boy. He just finished learning about germs in science class.

"I wonder if there are any germs at my school," thought Stan. "I don't want to get sick!"

1

"Children, it's time for lunch. Everyone line up to go to the restroom and wash your hands," said Mrs. Lemon, Stan's teacher.

"I want to be first in line," said Stan.

"Don't forget to wash your hands, everybody, so you don't get sick," said Mrs. Lemon.

"Psssh…I don't need to wash my hands. I never get sick!" stated Stan.

"You might want to rethink that, Stan," said a mysterious voice.

"Yikes! Who are you?" Stan stammered.

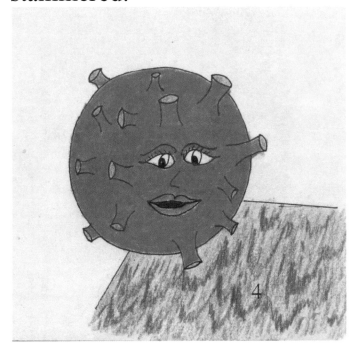

"Allow me to introduce myself. My name is *Roda* the Rotavirus," it said.

"What's a Rotavirus and what are you doing on my hands?" exclaimed Stan.

"I'm a virus. I go around and try to make people sick. If I got you sick, you would get uncontrollable diarrhea!" claimed Roda.

"Ew… How do I get rid of you?" Stan asked.

"Just wash your hands and I won't bother you anymore."

So be careful and don't get sick, Stan!

Lunchtime!! Stan is STARVING. He grabs a delicious pork chop from the lunch lady. Just as Stan was about to take a bite, he noticed a wormy looking face staring at him from his pork chop.

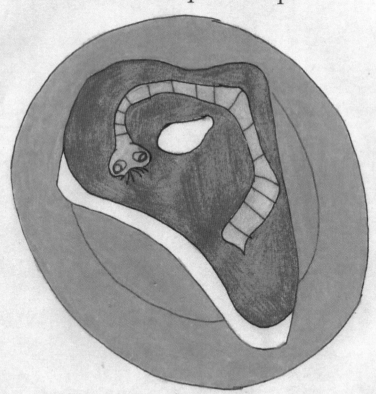

Stan exclaimed, "Who are you, and what are you doing in my pork chop?"

The worm said, "I am *Taenia solium*, but you can call me Tiny Taenia!"

"Well, how did you get here?"

"Okay, here's how it goes. The pork chop you're eating came from a pig. And the pig ate dirty food that had worm eggs. I hatched from my egg, and decided to live inside the pig's muscles.

The lunch lady was extra busy today and didn't cook your pork chop all the way. Otherwise, that would have gotten rid of me. So that's how I'm in your pork chop!" the worm explained.

"Well, you don't look like something I would want to live inside of me. What would you do to me?" Stan questioned.

Tiny Taenia replied, "See, that's the thing. You definitely don't want me to live inside of you. I wouldn't live in your muscles, instead I would live in your guts."

Stan gasped. "EWWW. Gross!"

"I have a special mouth to help me hold onto your intestines, and I have sharp, thorny spikes that hold me in place. So when you eat, I eat too. So we get to share!" Tiny Taenia grinned at Stan.

Stan stammered, "Well, exactly how much food are you going to eat... you're starting to look not so *tiny* anymore..."

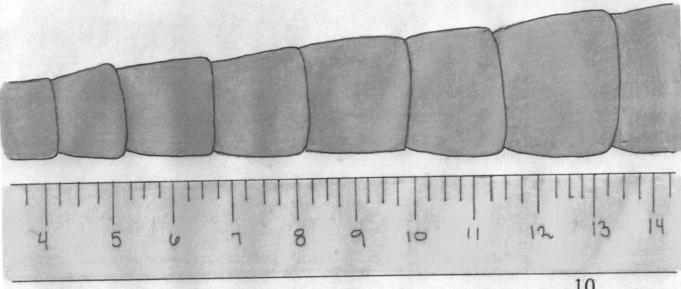

"Oh, I'll eat a lot. I can grow up to 20 feet long! That is taller than a house!"

"I'm not so hungry anymore…," Stan muttered. And he threw his pork chop and Tiny Taenia in the trash.

Watch out, and don't get sick, Stan!

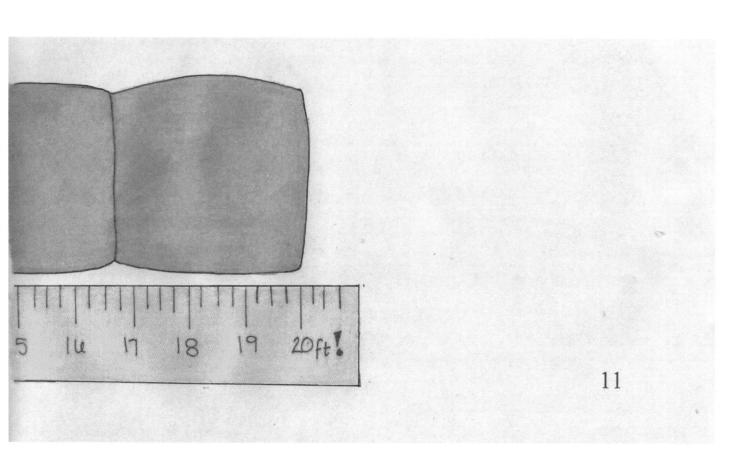

Stan continued on his way through the lunch line, but pushing his way to the front of the line was the school bully, Joe.

Towering behind Stan, he yelled, "Out of my way, loser!"

"I've had a bad day, Joe, just wait *your* turn," said Stan.

Joe laughed as he shoved Stan to the ground.

"How could this day get any worse?" Stan thought to himself.

12

Just then, he looked up to see apple juice being served. A smile returned to his face as he leaped to his feet.

"Oh boy! Juice boxes are my favorite!"

He snatched one and ran as fast as he could to a table. As he jammed the straw into the juice box, a splash of juice landed on his nose. "Surprise!" yelled something from his nose.

"Who are YOU?!" Stan questioned.

"My name is *Escherichia coli*, but my friends call me Ricky, and I live in the intestines of warm-blooded animals. You see, your juice was made from apples that are supposed to be picked from trees. However, some of the apples were picked up from the ground, where some poop can get on them, even though you won't see it. That's how I managed to make my way from the poop onto the apples.

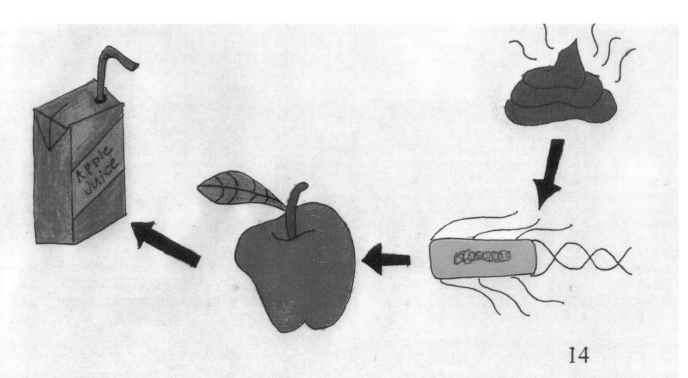

14

"Then they never heated the juice enough, and hot temperatures would make me go away. Now let me in, so that I may give you a tummy ache! Your gut is filled with all the stuff I love! Now drink your juice!"

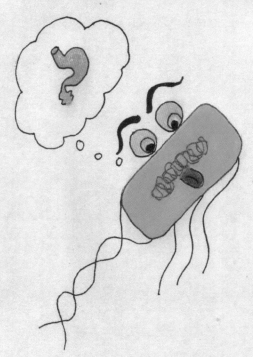

Stan, "I think I've had ENOUGH germs for today."

But look out, because there are MORE germs. Don't get sick, Stan!

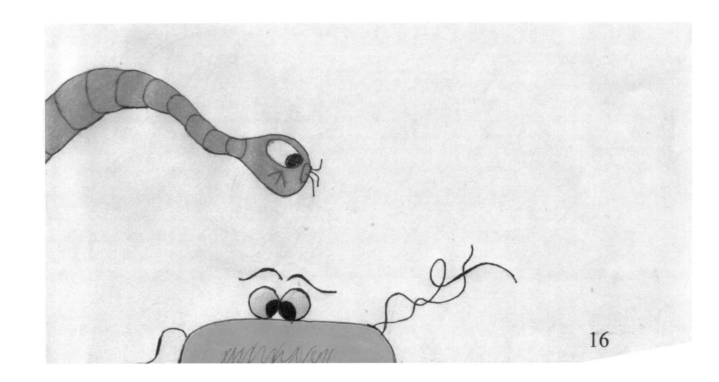

After lunch, Stan is outside at recess. He goes up to his teacher.

"Mrs. Lemon, I'm thirsty. I really need something to drink," said Stan.

"We will be going inside in about 10 minutes. You can get something then," she said.

"10 minutes! That's almost forever!" replied Stan.

"Oh! There are sprinklers over there!" thought Stan with a smirk.

He runs to them, about to drink, when he sees something small swimming in the water.

"Who are YOU?" asked Stan.

"I'm *Giardia lamblia*, or *Giardia* for short, and I live in dirty water."

"Are you going to try to make me sick, too?" asked Stan.

"Of course! I will give you diarrhea, and make you fart REALLY loudly!" *Giardia* stated proudly.

"So, how do I stop you from making me sick?" asked Stan.

"Well, you just need to drink clean water, and I won't make you sick," said *Giardia*.

So, drink water from the water fountains at school and the faucet at home, and don't get sick, Stan!

Stan finished recess and went home. He told his mom about all the germs he met today.

"I'm glad you learned so much. Now what should we do before dinner?" she asked.

"Wash our hands!" exclaimed Stan.

Even after a full day of school, Stan didn't get sick. He learned that he will avoid getting sick if he washes his hands, avoids contaminated food, and drinks clean water.

22

Pronunciation Guide

1) Rotavirus: ROW-ta-vi-rus	
2) *Taenia solium:* TEE-nee-ya SOW-lee-yum	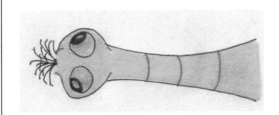
3) *Escherichia coli*: E-sher-REE-kee-ya CO-lie	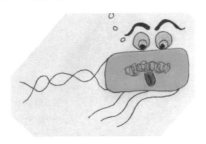
4) *Giardia lamblia*: Gee-YAR-dee-ya LAM-blee-ya	

23

Reviewers (Thank you!)

Dr. Samantha Alperin, Director of Undergraduate and Graduate Programs, Christian Brothers University, Memphis, TN

Sally Baer, Head of School, Bornblum Solomon Schechter School, Memphis, TN

Patricia J. Bump, APEX Instructor, Department of Exceptional Children, Shelby County Schools, TN

Dr. Roger Easson, Professor, Department of Literature and Languages, Christian Brothers University, Memphis, TN

Lisa Moore, FNP-C, Sheffield Pediatrics, Memphis, TN

Dr. Richard Potts, Chair, Director of Educational Leadership Programs

Dr. Richard Wanderman, M.D., Memphis, TN

Dr. William T. Weiss, M.D., Memphis, TN

Made in the USA
Charleston, SC
27 March 2012